Olympic DNA

Olympic DNA

Birth of the Fastest Humans

Rachael R. Irving

Acknowledgments

I am immensely grateful to the fantastic cadre of Jamaican athletes whose achievements are astounding, particularly Dr. Cynthia Thompson from the 1948 Olympics held in London, and Les Laing and Byron LaBeach, members of the 1952 team that set Jamaica's first world record. DNA sampling and personal histories from sprinting stalwarts underpin the foundation of information in *Olympic DNA*, which could not have been written without the athletes giving of themselves.

--R.R.I.

To God, the enabler of Jamaica's sprinting success:

you have timed my pen to produce a book

which truly speaks about the sprinting phenomenon.

--R.R.I.

<u>A Special Dedication</u>

To Whitney Houston, singing legend:

you have sprinted into heaven

after an amazing but exhausting life run

"I will always love you"

--R.R.I.

Contents

Introduction

Somewhere in St. James, Jamaica, lives a youngster whose poignant question gave birth to an idea that spurred the writing of *Olympic DNA: Birth of the Fastest Humans.* [1] He simply asked, "What is there to believe and inform my friends about as it relates to sprinting in Jamaica?" A kid who, after hearing various presentations at a seminar, wanted to know what more there was about sprinting in Jamaica, beyond boasting. He was tired of hearing about money and a way out of poverty being the motivating factors for Jamaica's sprinting prowess. He did not buy into the sprinting legacy claim, yet ironically he embodies the very legacy because he was born in Jamaica and more so in the Cockpit Country, a region of birth of many sprinting legends.

Therefore, the author of this book felt compelled, as a scientist, to examine oral histories relevant to sprinting and conceptualize the scientific analysis to understand the phenomenon. The analysis is profound, nevertheless the author presents it in such a way that sports fans can enjoy it.

For too long, we Jamaicans have been speaking about the transatlantic slave trade without analysing its lasting effect on the health of the transported people. For too long, we have ignored the impact of the Europeans who colonized the Caribbean shores. The descendants of Africans in the Americas, regardless of skin hue, cannot claim to be purebred Africans. Somewhere in the hull of the ships, there was a genetic shift, furthered by the environment of the plantations. The mystery is that somewhere between Africa and the Americas, there was a genetic adaptation, some heteroplasmy (mixing of normal and abnormal genes)

---

1   Cockpit Country is an area of Jamaica, so named because the barren bottom of its narrow valleys reminded the British, in colonial times, of cock fighting pits.

allowing a number of genes of our African ancestors to exert a multi-systemic role on the health and fitness of the progenies of those who survived the journey.

Rumours abound that the most aggressive, strongest of the slaves who were transported to Jamaica escaped to the Cockpit Country, an enclave of self government in the mountains of north central Jamaica. The fastest runners, the world record sprinters, the true Olympians are said to arise from that region. *Olympic DNA: Birth of the Fastest Humans* examines this claim.

The book also speaks to the kinship based on ethnic similarities between Jamaican and American sprinters. The biodata and sprinting styles of four sprinters or Cockpiters: Afasa Powell, Usain Bolt, Yohan Blake, and Tyson Gay are compared in: 2+1 ± An American. The author defined the American Tyson Gay as a Cockpiter because of his competitive spirit and the common ancestry of all black sprinters from the Americas. Olympic DNA offers an overview of the development of sprinting in the Americas, particularly Jamaica, from the time of the transatlantic slave trade to today.

1

The Transatlantic Slave Trade and Speed:

An Africana/Jamaican Story

The story

The performance of Jamaicans at the games of the 29th Olympiad in Beijing and the 12th IAAF World Championships in Athletics in Berlin has elicited cries of disbelief and amazement. Jamaica won six gold medals, three silver, and two bronze in Beijing and seven gold, four silver, and two bronze in Berlin. In 2011, at the 13th IAAF World Championships, Team Jamaica was distraught. There were widespread injuries in the camp in Daegu, South Korea. What made it worse is that anticipated star performer Usain Bolt had false started for the blue ribbon final, the 100-metre sprint. Like a phoenix, Yohan Blake took Usain's star-studded spot and became the youngest-ever male world champion at 100 metres. The 2008 Olympic and 2009 World Champion for the 400-metre hurdles, Melaine Walker, had a lacklustre performance during the 2011season due to injuries. Melaine was all but written off and was not expected to compete in the hurdles in Daegu. Throughout the rounds, Melaine competed with bandaged legs, barely limping into the final. She then took the bandages off and, with a superhuman effort, ran the race of her life, narrowly missing the gold. After the dust settled, the world was amazed that in spite of injuries, Jamaica had amassed nine medals, including four gold medals to emerge as one of the top performers in the sprints.

The sprinting legacy of Jamaica can be traced back almost seven decades, to 1948 when Dr. Cynthia Thompson, an unknown Jamaican woman, set an Olympic record in one of the heats of the 200-metre sprint. This tiny woman had arrived in London only days earlier, in the hull of a boat transporting bananas. This first Olympic record marked Jamaican sprinters propensity to achieve at the Olympic Games. In 2008, Jamaican Usain Bolt set three world records in the sprints at the Olympic Games. A year later, he demolished his 100-metre sprint world record. Scientists were bewildered at his time of 9.58 seconds, which was not expected to be achieved before another quarter century, based on data collected for more than a century.

The first Olympic record by a Jamaican woman was set by Dr. Cynthia Thompson

at the 1948 Olympics in London whilst wearing these shoes.

After setting three world records at the 2008 Olympics, Usain Bolt displayed his shoes.

The scientific study

In trying to answer the question, why do Jamaicans run so fast, the University of the West Indies in Jamaica and the University of Glasgow in Scotland researched the sprint phenomenon, with collaborative support from universities in Australia and the U.S. Two genes known to be related to performance, the actinin-3 (ACTN3) or "sprint gene" and the angiotensin converting enzyme gene (ACE), which is linked to respiration were investigated for their association with the sprint status of elite athletes from Jamaica. Some U.S. athletes were also studied so comparisons could be made because athletes from both nations are frequent contenders for Olympic and World titles. The genetic makeup (genotype) distributions of 116 Jamaican and 114 U.S. athletes were analysed and compared to those of ordinary Jamaicans and African Americans.

The sprint gene

Most persons of West African ancestry have the stronger 577RR or the weaker 577RX variant of the sprint gene. The 577RR genotype was found in 75% of Jamaican and 70% of U.S. athletes. Ordinary African Americans exhibited a 56% frequency of the 577RR genotype which is less than the frequency observed in the American athletes; however, ordinary Jamaicans have the same frequency of the 577RR as Jamaican athletes.

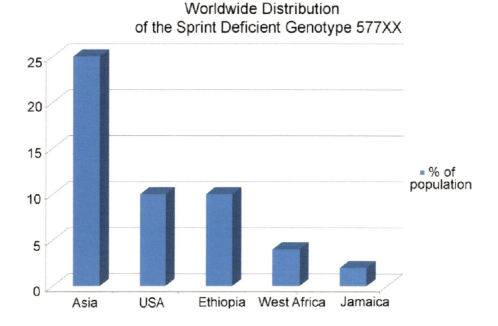

Only 2% of the Jamaican population lacks the sprint gene

The 577XX or deficient genotype, which does not produce the actinin protein associated with power sprinting, was found at a low frequency in African Americans and Jamaicans whether they were athletes or ordinary citizens (1). The XX genotype is usually absent in Olympic-calibre sprinters. Only about 1-4% of West Africans have it. In Jamaica, it is found in approximately 2% of the general population, compared to 25% in Asia, 18% in the U.S., and 10% in Ethiopia (East Africa) (1-2).

The making of the Jamaican sprinters

Approximately 75% of the Jamaicans tested have the 577RR, strong variant of the sprint gene. The big question is, can any three of four Jamaicans be a Usain Bolt or a Yohan Blake or a Veronica Campbell-Brown? Jamaicans, based on their shared ancestry with West Africans, are genetically predisposed to be sprinters, because the sprint gene frequency is high and similar in both regions. Many West Africans, however, are not performing as well as Jamaicans in international sprinting competitions. It is believed that the rigour of the transatlantic slave trade has caused some modifications to the genetic and metabolic profiles of those who survived (3), making them better able to function when oxygen is deficient. In some reports, between 50 and 96% of those transported died during the transatlantic journey. The progenies of those who survived tend to be masterful at the sprints. The sprint phenomenon can be associated with the Founder Effect where a small group from an original population carries genes from that population, but the genes are more robust and effective in the smaller pool. Based on this line of argument, the sprint gene may be more potent and directed in people of the Americas whose ancestors experienced the slave trade. Yohan Blake, purported to be of Yoruba, Mandinka, and Bantu descent, is the youngest male to win gold for the 100-metre sprint at the World Championships.

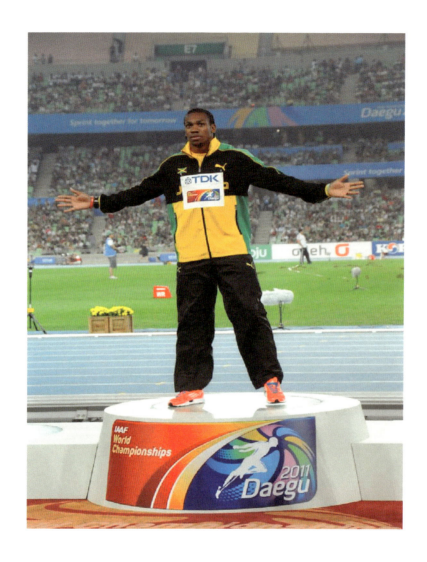

Yohan Blake, the youngest man ever to win the 100-metre sprint at the World Championships

Veronica Campbell-Brown was born in the Cockpit Country, which was once an enclave of defiant slaves known as the Maroons. She has won gold medals at all levels, steadily climbing the peaks of World Youth Championships, World Championships, and Olympic Games.

2004 Olympics: Veronica displaying her gold medal for the 200-metre sprint

2011 World Championships: Veronica Campbell defeated Carmelita Jeter of the U.S.

to win the 200-metre sprint

Historical records show that 49.9% of all Africans transported to Jamaica during the slave trade came out of Nigeria. The connection between Usain Bolt of Jamaica and Frank Obikwelu of Nigeria is uncanny. For years, scientists have believed that physiology determines pace. Research indicates that successful sprinters are usually between 173 and 190 cm in height. Only two elite sprinters, Frank Obikwelu and Usain Bolt fall outside the upper end of that range.

Physiology usually determines pace; heritable factors determine physiology.

The cheetah is the fastest land animal with a maximum speed of 75 mph.

The Jamaican Usain Bolt, with a speed of 27.79 mph, is the fastest man on earth.

A horse can reach a speed of 47.5 mph, between the cheetah and Usain Bolt.

Frank Obikwelu won silver in the 100-metre at the 2004 Olympics while competing for Portugal. His recorded time was 9.86 seconds. In the previous, 2000 Olympics, the gold was won in a time of 9.87 seconds. Usain Bolt, a progeny of transplanted West Africans, refined Obikwelu's effort. At the 2008 Olympics, he set world records of 9.69 seconds for 100 metres and 19.32 seconds for 200 metres to become the fastest living human.

The striking similarity between the Jamaican Usain Bolt and the Nigerian Frank Obikwelu

Metabolic adaptation

The ACE gene is associated with heart and lung function. There are three forms or variants of this gene (DI, DD, II) that are often linked to performance. The DI and DD forms are linked to sprinting and the II variant to endurance running (4). The study found that the percentages in Jamaican and U.S. athletes of the DI (52 vs 57) and DD (29 vs 32) variants of the ACE gene were similar. Jamaican athletes did not differ from ordinary Jamaicans in the ACE genotype frequency. U.S. male athletes differed from the general male population; they had a higher frequency of the DD variant. Scientific data indicate that athletes from the Americas, particularly males, use oxygen more efficiently. While exertion causes the production of lactic acid, which makes muscles sluggish, oxygenation counteracts this, therefore better oxygenation results in speedier recovery during successive rounds of competition (5). Men of the Americas seem better equipped to face the rigours of the heats to get to the 100-metre final. Since 1968, the battle for the Olympic gold in the 100-metre sprint has usually taken place between North American and Caribbean athletes. Consistently since 1984, the battle for the Olympic gold has been between Jamaican and U.S. athletes (Linford Christie and Donovan Bailey were born in Jamaica).

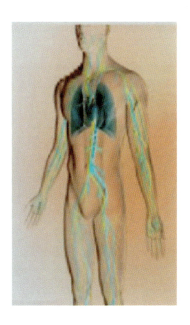

Rapid circulation of oxygen to muscles in athletes allows greater recovery during competition

Christophe Lemaitre might change the pattern. He is French, a Caucasian who has done remarkably well by breaking the European record for the 100-metre and placing a creditable fourth in the 100-metre final at the 2011 World Championships in Daegu. Neither the Founder Effect nor genetic adaptation may not hold in Lemaitre's case, however one anomaly does not mean that the overall pattern is incorrect. The world is watching to see how he holds out during the rounds of the 2012 Olympics and beyond.

Nurturing the natural talent of Jamaicans

The talent or sprinting trait might be inherited, but effective refinement is essential. Jamaica, like Brazil and Spain in football, or the U.S. and China in gymnastics, might be efficiently honing the talent of its nationals. The annual Boys and Girls Championships, in which Jamaican high school students compete, is akin to a mini sprint World Championship, and it prepares young talent for the world stage.

The annual Boys' and Girls' Championships hone young talent for the world stage.

Tremendous spectators' support during Boys' and Girls' Championships

The blessing and pitfalls

In regions of West Africa that are virtually untouched by modern civilization, heart disease is rare. One wonders whether this is the reason why the II variant of the ACE gene, associated with recovery from heart diseases, is low in persons of African descent.

The world is witnessing a population bottleneck effect of the transatlantic slave trade on people of the Americas. In the descendants, the way the body works has adapted to make more efficient use of oxygen with greater fueling of muscles but more stress on the heart and blood vessels, while there is a lower frequency of the II variant of the ACE gene to counter the extra stress. Less than 20% of the Jamaican and U.S. athletes that were tested had the II variant. It is no wonder that 35% of all retired Jamaican athletes are stricken with diabetes, hypertension, or some heart and blood vessels anomalies. The Afro-Americans are not spared. A disproportionate number has diabetes and hypertension, and they tend to die more from complications associated with heart diseases in comparison to Caucasians (6). Studies have linked cardiovascular complications to metabolic evolution used to counteract depletive diseases such as diarrhoea and hyperthermia during the transatlantic journey. Evolution can be compensatory but destructive. The people of the Americas whose ancestors survived the slave trade are arguably better sprinters than the descendants of Africans who were never exposed to this horror. With this pumped up sprinting talent comes increased disease in the Americas. Nature has a way of tempering greatness.

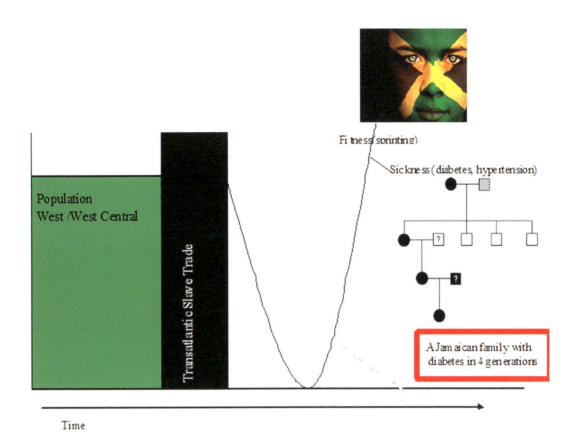

The Transatlantic Slave Trade and consequences on people of the Americas

References

1. Scott R, Irving R, Irwin L, Morrison M, Charlton V, Austin K, Tladi D, Headley A, Kolkhorst F, Yang N, North K, Pitsiladis P. ACTN3 and ACE Genotypes In Elite Jamaican and U.S. Sprinters. *Med Sci Sp Exer.* 2010; 42(1): 107-15.

2. Yang N, MacArthur D, Gulbin J, Hahn A, Beggs A, Easteal S, North K. *ACTN3* Genotype Is Associated With Human Elite Athletic Performance. *Am. J. Hum. Genet.* 2003; 73:627–631.

3. Wilson T, Grim C. Biohistory of Slavery and Blood Pressure Differences In Blacks Today. A Hypothesis. *Hypertension* 1991; 17(I): 122–28.

4. Amir O, Amir R, Yamin C, Attias E, Eynon N, Sagiv M, Sagiv M, Meckel Y. The *ACE* Deletion Allele Is Associated With Israeli Elite Endurance Athletes. *Exper. Physiology* 2007; 92: 881-6.

5. Morrison E, Cooper P. Some Biomedical Mechanisms In Athletic Prowess. *West Indies Medical J.* 2006; 55(3):205-9.

6. Maty S, James S, Kaplan G. Life-Course Socioeconomic Position and Incidence of Diabetes Mellitus Among Blacks and Whites: The Alameda County Study, 1965–1999. *American Journal of Public Health* 2010; 100(1): 137-45.

2

The Demographics of Jamaican Sprinters

A disproportionately high number of athletes from Ethiopia and Kenya dominate middle and long distance races at international meets. At the 2011 World Championships, Kenyans won five of the six marathon medals. The sixth was taken by Ethiopian Feyisa Lilesa. Jamaican athletes dominated the short distance races. Jamaicans won the men's 100-metre and 200-metre and women's 200-metre events and then bought the curtains down at the 13th IAAF World Championships in Athletics in explosive style with the championships' only world record; a fascinating 37.04 seconds run in the men's 4x100-metre relay.

It is widely known that there is a geographical imbalance in athletic representation in Ethiopia and Kenya. In Ethiopia, 38% of endurance runners are from the Arsi region which has less than 5% of the population. The Arsi and Shewa regions in the central highlands account for 73% of endurance runners. Eighty one percent of Kenyan international athletes are from the Rift Valley province which accounts for less than 25% of the Kenyan population. It has been postulated that geographical imbalance in athletic performance also exist in Jamaica with the majority of eli*te athletes reported to be from the Cockpit Country.*

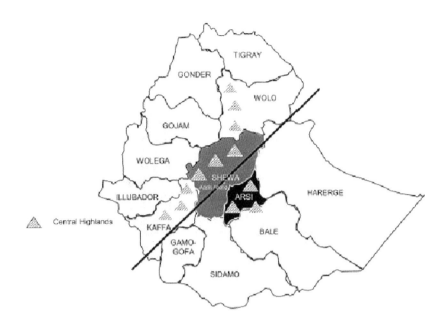

Map of the Central Highlands of Ethiopia – most Ethiopian elite endurance runners come from Arsi and

Shewa

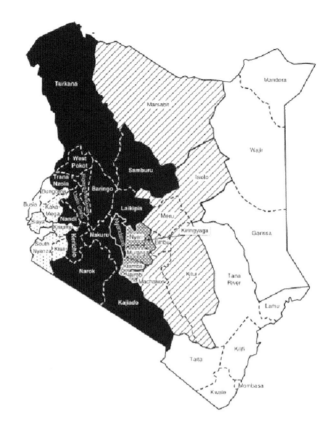

■ Rift Valley Province

*Provinces of Kenya showing the Rift Va*lley which accounts for 81% of Kenya's elite runners

Parishes and counties in Jamaica

Jamaica consists of fourteen parishes, namely Clarendon, Hanover, Kingston, St. Andrew, Manchester, Portland, St. Ann, St. Catherine, St. Elizabeth, St. James, St. Mary, St. Thomas, Trelawny, and Westmoreland which are distributed into three counties: Cornwall, Middlesex, and Surrey. **The Cockpit Country** area in Jamaica is a natural enclave where runaway slaves (Maroons) established communities while seeking refuge from the control of British rules. The Cockpit Country remains the largest area of intact wet limestone forest in Jamaica. There are different definitions of the boundaries based on geology (karst or limestone with sinks and ravines) or biology (resident life forms or endemic species). According to some definitions, the Cockpit Country is in north central Jamaica, mainly in the parish of Trelawny, but with areas in St. Elizabeth and St. James. Many persons loosely define the Cockpit Country as including areas of St. Ann and Manchester. Some of the descendants of runaway slaves still live in the Cockpit Country.

The Cockpit Country

To many, the Cockpit Country conjures up images of unspoiled, rugged terrain and clean air. For others, it is an area where escaped slaves called Maroons once controlled their own colony within the British colony. Maroons, during the time of slavery, had to be constantly on the lookout to avoid recapture by plantation owners, therefore they were always prepared to outrun and outgun the slave masters. The Maroons' descendants who were born in the Cockpit Country are said to have excellent control of their oxygen delivery system (VO_2 max utilization) and do not tire as easily as normal persons when running. Because of this theory and the prowess of Jamaicans at sprint meets, it is widely believed that most of Jamaican elite sprinters are from the Cockpit Country.

Places of birth of Jamaican elite athletes

Sport researchers from Scotland, the U.S. and Jamaica examined the claim that most of Jamaican elite athletes were born in the Cockpit Country by analysing the demographic data of 43 elite athletes who had medalled at World Championships and Olympics Games. The chart of medallists by parish of birth shows that most were born in the parish of Kingston—not in the Cockpit Country. When the parishes of St. James, St. Elizabeth, and Trelawny, which constitute the Cockpit Country, were combined, the total number of athletes from that area who medalled at the World and Olympic Games was far lower than the number of athletes born in Kingston. When the parishes of St. Ann and Manchester, sometimes mistakenly called Cockpit area, were merged with the Cockpit Country and the number of medallists born in all five parishes (St. James, St. Elizabeth, Trelawny, St. Ann, and Manchester) was tallied, the total was marginally higher than that of Kingston (13 versus 10). By county, Middlesex (see map of Jamaica) had the most medallists (17) at the Olympic Games and World Championships. Middlesex is made up of the parishes of St. Catherine, St. Mary, St. Ann, Manchester, and Clarendon and is the largest (5042 km²) of the three counties. The county of Surrey consisting of Kingston, Portland, St. Andrew, and St. Thomas although smallest (2,009 km²), had the second highest number (14) of medallists at the Olympic Games and World Championships. Approximately 28% of all medallists came out of the county of Surrey. The county of Cornwall with 3,939 km² and consisting of the parishes of St. James, Trelawny, St. Elizabeth, Westmoreland and Hanover, had the least number of medallists (12).

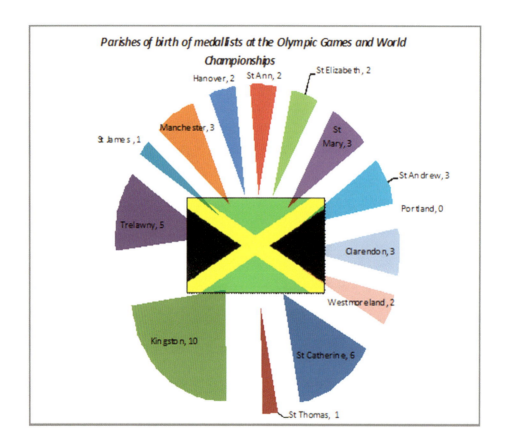

The number of athletes medalling from each parish in Jamaica

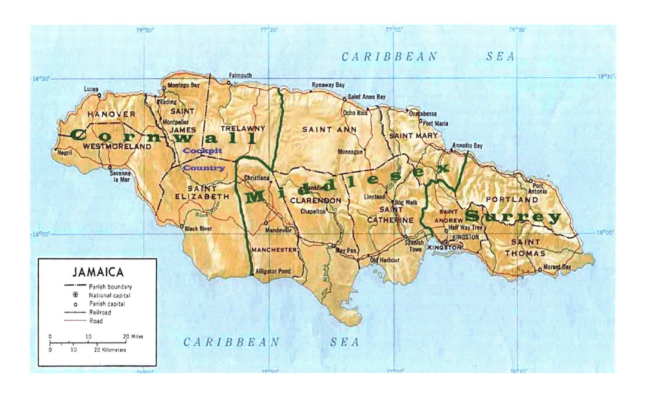

Map of Jamaica showing the counties and the Cockpit Country

Conclusion

Jamaica's sprint population is distributed all over the island, unlike endurance runners from Ethiopia and Kenya who are overrepresented in certain areas, namely Arsi and Shewa in Ethiopia and the Rift Valley in Kenya. In each of the three counties of Jamaica, there is a particular parish from where most of the county's elite sprinters emerged. It is Kingston for Surrey, St Catherine for Middlesex, and Trelawny for Cornwall.

One of the greats from the Cockpit County: Yohan Blake after winning the 100-metre at the 2011 World Championships in Daegu, South Korea

Jamaica's most outstanding sprinters Usain Bolt, triple world record holder, Yohan Blake, youngest ever 100-metre world champion, and Veronica Campbell-Brown, the only woman to have consistently medalled at the Youth and World Championships and Olympic Games, were born in the Cockpit Country. Outstanding sprint talents do emerge particularly from the Cockpit Country.

References

1. Scott R, Georgiades E, Wilson R, Goodwin W, Wolde B, Pitsiladis Y. Demographic Characteristics of Elite Ethiopian Endurance Runners. *Medicine & Science in Sports and Exercise* 2003: 1727-32.

2. Onywera I, Robert S, Boit M, PitsiladisY. Demographic Characteristics of Elite Kenyan Endurance Runners. *Journal of Sports Sciences* 2006; 24(4): 415–22.

3

Jamaican and U.S. Sprinters Are Distant Cousins

The sprint factory

The presence and increasing dominance of Jamaicans in international sprinting events remain largely unexplained. Joseph McKenzie ignited the torch in 1930 with a silver medal in the high jump at the Central American and Caribbean Games as Jamaica entered its first-ever athletics team in an international competition. In 1948, just three years after the second world war, this pre-independence nation of people who are mainly descendants of recent slaves from Africa stunned the sporting world by winning one gold and two silver medals at the Olympics in London. In 1952, Helsinki stood in amazement as the quartet of Herb McKenley, Arthur Wint, Leslie Laing, and George Rhoden defeated the mighty U.S. team to set a world record of 3:03:9 in the 4 x 400-metre. Three of the men from the quartet contributed four individual medals to Jamaica's tally. The nation still then under direct colonial dictates finished a remarkable 13th in the medal table, ahead of its colonizer, Great Britain. Post Independence, almost six decades later in 2008, another relay world record was set, this time for the 4 x 100-metre by a new generation of Jamaican men. Jamaicans won five of the six possible gold medals in the sprints at the 2008 Olympics and again finished 13th in the medal table. Yet again in 2011, a third quartet of Jamaican men set a world record for the 4 x 100-metre sprint. Jamaicans contribute to the sprint medal tally not only for their country but also for other countries. Many former world record holders and Olympic medallists, such as Linford Christie and Germaine Mason of Great Britain, Donovan Bailey and Charmaine Crooks of Canada, and Sanya Richards-Ross of the U.S. were born in Jamaica but migrated as children. The direct descendants of Jamaicans who delivered medals from World Championships and Olympic Games to the nations which they were transplanted have also been astounding. Kelly Holmes, whose father originated from Jamaica, has seized two Olympic gold medals for Great Britain. Denise Lewis, whose mother came from the parish of Hanover in Jamaica, won gold for Great Britain at the Olympics in 2000. Both parents of Colin Jackson, the World Championships hurdler of Great Britain, are from Jamaica. The mother of the Olympian Ato Boldon of Trinidad is from Jamaica. Southern Europe was not untouched, as Italian World Games champion Fiona May has a parent of Jamaican origin. Some people strongly believe that Jamaica is the sprint factory of the world.

Usain Bolt, Nesta Carter and Asafa Powell celebrating after setting a world record for 4 x 100-metre at the

2008 Olympics in Beijing

Human movement and sprinting

How does the movement or translocation of people from one continent to another affect sprinting? Tracing the anthropology of recent human movement in sports, particularly athletics, we can reasonably deduce that people of the Americas (the U.S., Jamaica, the rest of the Caribbean) dominate sprinting. What is undeniable is the presence of Jamaicans in the sprint finals of Olympic Games and World Championships. The men's 100-metre final at the 2008 Beijing Olympics featured three Jamaicans: Usain Bolt, Michael Frater, and Asafa Powell. The final of the women's 100-metre in Beijing was dominated by Jamaicans in a 1.2.2 finish by Shelly Ann Frazer, Kerron Stewart, and Sherone Simpson.

1.2.2 finish for the Jamaican ladies in the 100-metre sprint at the 2008 Olympics

Americans and other nationals from Caribbean countries, such as Trinidad and Tobago and the former Netherlands Antilles also performed prominently in the Olympics of 2008. Whilst Jamaican men won the gold medals at the 2009 and 2011 World Championships, American men were in second place on the heels of the Jamaicans. Anthropological studies indicate that most of these sprinters of the Americas are from West Africa or west central Africa (1). The fact that Jamaicans and Americans of West African descent have such a strong presence in the recent finals of international sprint events, along with the historical sprint rivalry between Jamaica, a small nation, and the more developed U.S. have led to many scientific speculations. These speculations are fuelled by data such as the sprint progeny of slave progenies of Jamaican soil setting numerous world records for the Americas. Michael Johnson's grandparents were born in the county of Middlesex, Jamaica which to date has produced the greatest number of Jamaican medallists at the World Championships and Olympic Games.

Country (flag) by year of men who have held the 100-metre world record

The hypothesis seems to be the following: The elite sprinters of the Americas, particularly Jamaica and the U.S., are from the same general pool of ancestors pool. History had witnessed the spreading of descendants of Africans in the Americas with some concentrated in southern U.S. states, and others distributed in Jamaica and other regions of the Caribbean.

The Jamaica-U.S. nexus

The battle for supremacy between Jamaica and the U.S. sprinters and the associated heightened passion in both nations have forced the author of this book to analyse the ancestral relationships between sprinters of the two countries. The focus of this book is on the U.S. and Jamaica because of the sheer number of representatives from these two nations in sprint finals at the Olympics and World Championships, nevertheless sprinters from other areas of the Americas such as the Bahamas, Trinidad and Tobago, and Antigua are sometimes present in the elite sprint finals.

Population stratification, the increasing presence of sprinters of West African ancestry on the podium, the raw prowess of U.S. and Jamaican athletes in the short sprints at World Championships and Olympic Games have led the author to try to answer a puzzling question:

Are elite sprinters of the Americas (the U.S., Jamaica, the rest of the Caribbean) from the same ancestral origin?

Three Jamaicans and two Americans competed in the final of the 100-metre sprint at the 2008 Olympics

Elite sprinters from the Americas

Elite sprinters of the Americas are defined as sprinters who have won a gold, silver, or bronze medal at the Olympic Games or World Championships or both. We can name a few elite sprinters from the Americas: Donovan Bailey, Yohan Blake, Ato Boldon, Usain Bolt, Linford Christie, Ana Fidelia, Shelly Ann Frazer, Tyson Gay, Michael Johnson, Merlene Ottey, Asafa Powell, and Cynthia Thompson. All of them appear to be of West African ancestry. A common means of tracing ancestry is by analysing mitochondrial DNA. Mitochondrial DNA is passed from mother to child and it is easier to trace lineage using DNA passed from the maternal side. Mitochondrial DNA (mtDNA) is passed on without changes except for rare, spontaneous mutation. These changes can be used to back trace populations of people to a distant common ancestor, thus maternal ancestry can be traced to a particular area of the globe. Scientists have used these traces to pinpoint American and Caribbean population origins to regions of west and west central Africa (2-3). Family trees have been created and members identified using mitochondrial DNA. Mitochondrial DNA analysis done on elite sprinters of the Americas indicated the presence of haplotypes or markers from West Africa (1). The common markers L1b, L2e, L3e, and L3f found in the DNAs of Jamaica and U.S. sprinters are potent indicators of recent shared ancestry.

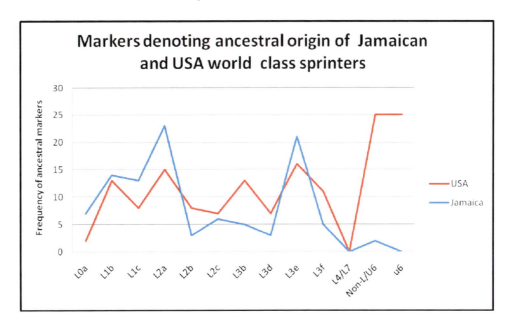

Jamaican and U.S. elite sprinters share many common ancestral markers of West Africa (L1b, L2a,L3e, L3f) however the European influence on U.S. athletes is striking (Non-L/U6) and minimal at most on the Jamaican athletes. North Africa (L4/L6) had no influence on the two groups. Asian influence on both groups is almost non-existent.

Conclusion

Jamaican and U.S. sprinters are from the same ancestry in West Africa and may in fact be distant cousins.

References

1. Deason M, Scott R, Irwin L, Macaulay V, Fuku N, Tanaka M, Irving R, Charlton V, Morrison E, Austin K, Pitsiladis P. Importance of Mitochondrial Haplotypes and Maternal Lineage In Sprint Performance Among Individuals of West African Ancestry. *Scand J Med Sci Sports* 2011. Doi: 10.1111/j.1600-0838.2010.01289.x

2. Salas A, Richards M, De la Fe T, Lareu M, Sobrino B, Sanchez-Diz P, Macaulay V, Carracedo A. The Making of the African mtDNA Landscape. *Am. J. Hum. Genet.* 2002; 71:1082–111.

3. Salas A, Richards M, Lareu M, Scozzari R, Coppa A, Torroni A, Macaulay V, Carracedo A. The African Diaspora: Mitochondrial DNA and the Atlantic Slave Trade. *Am. J. Hum. Genet.* 2004; 74:454 –65.

4

The Cockpiters: 2+1± An American

1.90 m, born 11/23/1982

Asafa Powell

1.96 m, born 08/21/1986

*Usain Bol*t

1.80 m, born 12/26/1989

Yohan Blake

Born to run

Jamaica continues to produce outstanding sprinters. Three men come readily to mind: Asafa Powell, Usain Bolt, and Yohan Blake. Seeing their deeds, the world had to take a second glance. In this book, some basic performance parameters of these men were examined and a scientific analysis of performance traits in a comparative mode was attempted. The attempted analysis is based on genetic studies of the men, phenotypic evaluation of sprinting styles, and psychological profiles observed during competition. Two of the men, Usain Bolt and Yohan Blake, were born in the Cockpit Country, a remote region in Jamaica once controlled by defiant slaves called Maroons. The Maroons had to keenly listen to the winds and the birds because any unusual sounds might have indicated imminent capture. Sprinting during slavery meant survival and this is still true today. The third man, Asafa, like Usain and Yohan, was born in Jamaica but in a different region, the parish of St. Catherine, an area once controlled by plantation owners. The writer makes no scientific claim that parish or county of birth in Jamaica affects prowess but wishes to point out the effect on the attitude of the competitor. Just as a child learns from the environment and adopts the attitude of parents, oral tradition is powerful in Jamaica. The Maroons have been passing down beliefs and attitudes through generations, and today, they remain the only autonomous group within Jamaica. The great Herb McKenley who led the way for the younger generation of sprinters once remarked, "Science without history is useless." If we can accept the theory that people of African descent dominate running with a predominance of persons of West African descent commandeering sprinting, then it is feasible to believe that finer genetic traits or small regional differences are important. There will always be good sprinters from the Americas because of genetic pre-disposition; there will sometimes be better sprinters from Jamaica because of cultural exposition but somewhere, somehow amongst them, the best sprinter will always rise to the top of the pile. Something must be differentiating this sprinter from the others. Do we dare to think that birth in the Cockpit Country can make the difference amongst the good, the better and the best? The writer mentioned Tyson Gay, an extraordinary American sprinter, and attempted a minor comparison with the three Jamaican sprinting stars because Tyson Gay's American Record of 9.69 seconds for the 100-metre stands somewhere between Asafa Powell's former world record of 9.74 seconds and Usain Bolt's world record of 9.58 seconds. Additionally, studies indicate that Tyson may be from the same region of West Africa as Asafa, Yohan, and Usain. The title of this chapter, 2 +1±An American speaks to the profiles of "2" men, Usain Bolt and Yohan Blake, from the Cockpit Country, "+1," Asafa Powell also from Jamaica, the reputed sprint capital of the world, "± An American," Tyson Gay of West African ancestry like the three Jamaican men.

Profiles

<u>Asafa Powell</u>

World record, Reiti Italy, 9th September 2007

Asafa best fits the profile of the classical elite sprinter. He is about 1.90 metres tall which puts him at the upper end of the height range for top class sprinters (1.73-1.90 metres). His usual Body Mass Index (BMI) of approximately 23.5 kg/m² is well within normal indices, giving him the structural stability to effectively execute his sprint. Additionally, he is a fine starter who goes into the drive phase of his race efficiently.

Pictures of the legs of four of the fastest sprinters in the world

Asafa Powell in yellow sneakers, second from the left is the most centred of the men during the drive phase. His leading leg is directed, giving him the stability to sprint almost in a straight line (180^0). A straight line is the shortest distance to any destination therefore the more linear the sprint the quicker the sprinter reaches the finish line.

Individual world records:

1. 100-metre (9.77 seconds), Athens Greece; 2005

2.100-metre (9.74 seconds), Reiti Italy; 2007

Usain Bolt

Usain's height of 1.96 metres is outside the range of the normal sprinters (1.73-1.90m). Usain had a BMI of approximately 24.7 kg/m^2 at the time of the 2009 World Championships when he set the world record of 9.58 seconds. A BMI greater than 24.6 kg/m^2 is unusual for sprinters who set world records. He is presently more muscular and lighter at a BMI of about 23.9 kg/m^2 which is more similar to that of Asafa Powell and the American Tyson Gay. Usain Bolt is not the smoothest of starters. He was the second slowest starter at the 2008 Beijing Olympics with a reaction time of 0.165 second, yet he managed not only to overtake his competitors, but danced while setting a world record of 9.69 seconds for 100 metres. At the 2011 World Championships, he did the unforgivable: false started for the 100-metre final. Although Usain often shows deficiencies at the start of his race, by mid-race he generates enough elastic energy, and he shows flexibility in the hip flexors to allow superb hip extension at toe-off, therefore he is able to maintain his marvellous stride length during competition. He is a stride-length-dependent athlete. His stride length allows him to be about 12% more efficient over 100 metres when compared with average-height competitors.

Individual world records

1. 100-metre world record (9.72 seconds), Reebok Grand Prix in New York; 2008

2 100-metre (9.69 seconds), 200-metre (19.30 seconds), Beijing Olympics, China; 2008

3. 100-metre (9.58 seconds), Berlin, Germany; 2009

4. 200-metre (19.19 seconds), Berlin, Germany; 2009

Usain Bolt is so good at toe-off that he can break to have fun while setting a world record for the 100-metre sprint.

<u>Yohan Blake</u>

Yohan Blake is 1.80 metres tall with a BMI of approximately 24.1 kg/m^2. Yohan's strength in running is generated from muscular bulk. He has a powerful force production during the contact phase, which gives him a bounce upward from the ground, along with good hip flexibility, so that he is able to produce long strides. His average height of 1.80 metres and bulk do not allow him to be as elastic as Usain, however Yohan's powerful force production lifts him off the ground and allows him to go very fast.

Yohan's powerful force production lifts him off the ground and allows him to go fast

Yohan Blake strides away from his competitors in the 100-metre at the 2011 World Championships

Psychology and effects on weaknesses

Beautiful start but dreadful finish

Asafa usually looks tense during competition. Fine sprinting involves symbiosis of neural and muscular functions. Mental fortitude sometimes determines success when conditions are difficult. Asafa has trained himself to lose. The fastest ever relay leg of the 4 x 100-metre is 8.70 seconds done by Asafa Powell in 2008. Asafa is one of the fastest starters of the sub-10-second sprinters, yet he usually fades toward the finish line in the "big" races. There is no reason for Asafa to run out of steam towards the 100-metre post, since energy from the glycolytic pathway is available for at least 10 seconds. Asafa has done enough sub-10-seconds to program his glycolytic pathway to fire effectively during a race, however he has deprogrammed the firing of his neurotransmitters by giving up to his competitors at about 65 metres. Asafa should practice closing out his competitors towards or at the winning line and not only at the start. The cycle of breaking down towards the end can be repaired via proper channelling of his adrenaline by him staying focused and maintaining linearity as competitors close in. The race is usually lost by Asafa after 65 metres and convincingly after 80 metres.

Horrific start, magnificent recovery

The scientific literature tells you that sprinting prowess starts declining after age 25 years. Usain was born in 1986. Usain has had constant bouts with scoliosis which might affect sprinting posture and precipitate some sort of early immunosenescence (system aging), however Usain's superb mental control and probably high level of the neurotransmitter serotonin have allowed him to will his structure to be as elastic as possible in competition. His strides tend to be longer near the end of the race as his mental fortitude forces physical adjustment. Science tells you that with Usain's build, he should not be going that fast (27.79 mph). The scientists did not take into consideration Usain's mental control.

The imagery sprinter

Yohan can be classified as an emotional sprinter. Examine his face as he runs: sprinting ideation is most real. The will to win is seen in his whole demeanour. However, this can sometimes be counterproductive when he gets too emotionally caught up in his race, thus losing the core stability which drives his race. By the 2013 World Championships, Yohan would have learnt what it means to control the sounds and innuendos of his emotion to achieve his prowess. His ancestors the Maroons did it during slavery–like them, he will learn to develop fine neural control.

Tyson Gay

Many might ask, why compare Tyson Gay with the Jamaicans if the goal is to examine the performance traits of three outstanding men of Jamaican soil? Place of birth can be only relatively different when distant ancestry is mostly similar. If we come from the premise that the four men's ancestors were from a common region with biological markers that indicate kinship, then we should expect some similarity amongst them. These men may be described as extraordinary sprinters of the Americas of West African descent who have excelled at the Olympic Games and World Championships. Tyson, because he is non-Jamaican, tries hard. The psyche of the Americans rests on his shoulders because he has never been able to compete effectively with his "cousin" Usain from Jamaica. At the 2009 World Championships, he did 9.71 seconds for the 100-metre. However, Usain was able to close him out by dipping lower, to 9.58 seconds. Tyson is sandwiched between Usain and Asafa.

Tyson closing out Asafa for the silver but unable to match the strides of Usain

for the gold at the 2009 World Championships

By mental strategies, he has many times closed out Asafa when Asafa is far superior in terms of sprinting style and reach. Tyson shows the spirit of a Cockpiter even though he is not from the Cockpit Country.

Tyson stands at 1.80 metres with a usual BMI of 23.1 kg/m^2, which puts him on the lighter side of the profile of the average sprinters. He overworks to generate elastic energy and appears to lack flexibility in the hip flexors to allow good hip extension at toe-off, thus giving him the most flawed sprinting style when compared with Asafa, Usain, and Yohan. Like Usain, Tyson is able to defeat Asafa and other great competitors because he is mentally savvy.

To correct his inflexibility, Tyson had hip impingement or shaving done. The world is waiting to see if he, as the oldest of the four men, will be able to surpass the feats of his cousin Usain or deflate the ego of an even younger cousin Yohan or continues to break the will of his comparative aged cousin Asafa . The Cockpiters: 2+1± An American whether by birth, kinship, or prowess are four of the best sprinters from the Americas.

Photo and Illustration Credits

All photos courtesy of the Jamaica Observer with the exception of the following: Shoes of Dr. Cynthia Thompson by David Miguel; Usain Bolt and Frank Obikwelu by Senia Burrell; Rapid Circulation from iStockphoto; Map of Ethiopia by Yannis Pitsiladis; Map of Kenya from I. Onywera/*Journal of Sport Science*; Map of Jamaica by David Miguel; View of the Cockpit Country by Parris Ayee; Asafa Powell courtesy of Yannis Pitsiladis; Asafa and the world record courtesy of Yannis Pitsiladis; Feet of athletes by Senia Burrell; Usain Bolt, Tyson Gay, and Yohan Blake by David Miguel.

Made in the USA
Charleston, SC
13 April 2012